Queen Elizabeth

A Platinum Jubilee Celebration

Contents

On a February day 70 years ago,
a young princess suddenly found out
that she was now a queen. Today, she is still
our reigning monarch, and in 2022 we are celebrating
the record-breaking Platinum Jubilee of Queen Elizabeth II.
During her reign, the world has changed in so many ways,
but she has stayed strong and steady throughout;
a calm, confident, kind presence in all our lives.

You are receiving this book to commemorate this once-in-a-lifetime,
memorable moment. It will help you understand the amazing life
and times of our Queen and the magic of the unique, unshakable
bond she shares with the people she serves. You'll discover the
rich history of the UK and Commonwealth and meet a few of
the incredible achievers who have helped to make the 70 years
of The Queen's reign so eventful and extraordinary.

The Platinum Jubilee not only honours Her Majesty's long and
loyal service, but also the resilient, diverse, and inclusive communities
that we live in. It is a time for us all to come together – and celebrate!

This book belongs to:

....

Chapter One
Coronation and Commonwealth

"Isabella, do you know anything about the Jubilee?"

Isabella was at her Great Granny Joyce's house. She loved to visit every Sunday to hear her amazing stories. She had just settled down with a slice of fruitcake when Great Granny Joyce started talking about the Jubilee. This was a new word for Isabella, and she didn't have a clue what it meant.

"No I don't, Great Granny Joyce," Isabella admitted, through a mouthful of cake crumbs. "What is it?"

Great Granny Joyce clapped her hands together in delight and sat forward in her chair.

"It's a special celebration and lots of people will be talking about it. There will be Jubilee programmes on the TV, and there will be so many festivities taking place across the UK, with street parties, barbecues, and afternoon teas – all kinds of events!"

Isabella smiled. "Well, I do love a celebration! But who is it actually for?"

By now, Great Granny Joyce's eyes were twinkling.
They always twinkled when she was excited.

Great Granny Joyce opened her eyes wider. "It's for The Queen!"
She got up from her chair and announced, "This year, in 2022,
Queen Elizabeth II will have reigned for 70 years, so we're
going to celebrate this anniversary as the Platinum Jubilee!
It's a milestone for Her Majesty!"

Isabella considered this for a moment and did some
quick maths in her head. "I'm nine years old, so that means
The Queen reigned for 61 years before I was even born! Wow!"

"Wow, goodness me!" agreed Great Granny Joyce. "I'm 96 years old this
year – exactly the same age as The Queen. I remember so much of her reign."

Suddenly, Great Granny Joyce stood still and her eyes misted up.
"It takes me back to my youth... Isabella, I want to show you something
very special. Wait here."

Great Granny Joyce returned carrying a big, wooden box and
Isabella jumped up to help. They set it down on the rug.

"You can open it now," said Great Granny Joyce.

With trembling fingers, Isabella opened
the lid very slowly and carefully...

Isabella pushed the lid of the box back as far as it would go and looked inside. The box was packed with all kinds of things. There were souvenirs from holidays, tickets to shows, letters from friends, birthday cards, certificates, postcards, newspaper cuttings, trinkets, toys, and so many photographs. Isabella didn't know what to look at first.

"My entire life's experiences are in that box," said Great Granny Joyce, looking over Isabella's shoulder. "I started collecting things as a child – things that I've picked up here and there. Some are memories of the best days I've ever had, others are souvenirs saved for rainy days. It's all here in one place. I call it my Treasures Box."

Isabella started to look through the mass of memories. There was so much to take in. Then she spotted something special that caught her eye.

"Wait! Who is this?" Isabella pulled out a stunning photograph of a young lady wearing a crown.

Isabella waved the photograph under her
Great Granny Joyce's nose, waiting for her to answer.

"That's The Queen, when she was much younger.
It was taken at her Coronation in the summer of 1953."

Isabella's ears pricked up. Coronation? This sounded like a magical
word, but she couldn't quite put her finger on what it meant.
"What was the Coronation, Great Granny Joyce?"

"The Coronation was the ceremony to mark Princess Elizabeth
becoming Queen. It was the first Coronation to be shown on TV.
Not everyone had TVs back then. But those that did, or knew
someone who did, tuned in to watch it."

Great Granny Joyce stared at the picture for a long time.
"Can you believe it? Seventy years! So long ago – but I
remember it like it was yesterday."

"But why do you have a picture of the Coronation? Shouldn't this be
in The Queen's Treasures Box, not yours?" Isabella asked in confusion.

Great Granny Joyce gave her great granddaughter a hug.

"My Treasures Box is personal to me and our family, but a lot
of it is also about the Royal Family. I was born in the same year
as The Queen, so I feel like I have grown up with Her Majesty.
The Coronation was for everyone to celebrate; we were all part
of it. This was our new Queen and we felt so proud of her. That
memory is part of my history, too. There are plenty more souvenirs
of the Coronation in my Treasures Box. Let me show you..."

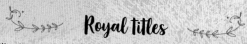

Royal titles

Queen Elizabeth II has been known by this name in most parts of the UK since February 1952 when she became Queen. However, in Scotland, she is referred to as Her Majesty The Queen. This is because Elizabeth I was only Queen of England and never ruled Scotland. Around the world, The Queen has a number of different royal titles. For example, Queen Elizabeth II is named Queen of Australia in Australia, Queen of Jamaica in Jamaica, and Duke of Normandy in the Channel Islands.

Coronation ceremony

Look, I made a scrapbook of the Coronation with different articles and souvenirs. Have a read, Isabella. It'll be just like you were there!

The Coronation of Queen Elizabeth II took place on 2 June 1953. Thousands of people lined the streets of London, while 11 million people all across the UK listened on the radio, and about 20 million people watched on television.

The day unfolded like a fairy tale. All the staff at Buckingham Palace waited inside the Grand Hall to see The Queen and her husband, His Royal Highness The Prince Philip, Duke of Edinburgh, depart for Westminster Abbey. The couple travelled from Buckingham Palace to Westminster Abbey in the Gold State Coach, which was pulled by eight horses. Crowds cheered as the royal coach made its way along the streets of London. People camped overnight all the way along The Mall to get the best view of the couple as they passed. Some people even sailed all the way from Australia just to be there for the big occasion!

I wish I could have been there. Imagine the things I'd have heard and seen, and all the people I'd have met!

The Queen and Prince Philip entered Westminster Abbey for the ceremony, which was led by the Archbishop of Canterbury, and which lasted almost three hours. In the congregation was The Queen's eldest son, Charles, who had received a hand-painted children's invitation. He was the only one of The Queen's children at the Coronation because his younger sister, Anne, was a toddler and considered too young to go. Precisely 8,251 people from all over the world attended the Coronation, with a total of 129 nations and territories officially represented.

The Queen was crowned in St Edward's Chair, a special seat handcrafted in 1300 for Edward I of England. St Edward's Crown, made of solid gold in 1661, was placed on The Queen's head. Her Majesty became the 39th ruler to be crowned at Westminster Abbey.

Since that memorable day, The Queen has worn the Coronation Dress on six more occasions, including to open the parliaments of New Zealand and Australia in 1954.

So how do the different nations of the UK fit together?

Royal gown

The Queen wore a gown of white satin, embroidered with floral designs. Before the St Edward's Crown was placed on The Queen's head, she wore the Diamond Diadem, which is the crown you see on UK postage stamps. This crown features roses, thistles, and shamrocks to represent England, Scotland, and Northern Ireland, as well as 1,333 diamonds and 169 pearls. The Queen carried a bouquet of flowers that included orchids and lilies of the valley from England, stephanotis from Scotland, orchids from Wales, and carnations from Northern Ireland and the Isle of Man.

Just look at The Queen's gown, made especially for the Coronation!

Let me show you. I have a map somewhere...

The UK

Our nation is officially called the United Kingdom of Great Britain and Northern Ireland – or simply the UK for short. It is made up of four parts – England, Scotland, Wales, and Northern Ireland, nations with histories stretching back more than a thousand years. London is the capital city of both England and the UK.

> Isabella, the UK is made up of four nations, including England, where we live.

Union flag

The flag of the UK is more widely known as the Union Jack. It is made up of three flags – the red cross of St George for England, the white diagonal cross of St Andrew for Scotland, and the red diagonal cross of St Patrick to represent Ireland, although only Northern Ireland is part of the UK. Wales does not feature in the flag because the flag was created when Wales was, at that time, part of the Kingdom of England.

Scotland

Northern Ireland

England

Wales

> Oh! I see now. They fit like pieces of a jigsaw.

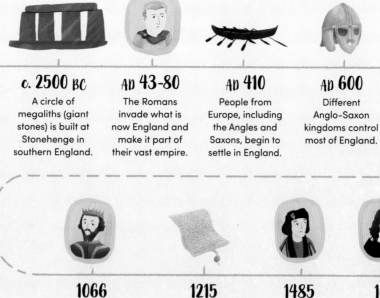

c. 2500 BC
A circle of megaliths (giant stones) is built at Stonehenge in southern England.

AD 43-80
The Romans invade what is now England and make it part of their vast empire.

AD 410
People from Europe, including the Angles and Saxons, begin to settle in England.

AD 600
Different Anglo-Saxon kingdoms control most of England.

AD 793
Vikings from Scandinavia raid the monastery on the Island of Lindisfarne.

England

England is in the southern part of Great Britain – the geographical name for the island that is home to Scotland, England, and Wales. By area, England is the largest part of the UK and home to about 84 per cent of the UK population.

1066
William of Normandy becomes King of England after the Battle of Hastings.

1215
Magna Carta states that the monarch must also obey the laws of the land.

1485
Henry Tudor becomes Henry VII after the Wars of the Roses.

1649
After the English Civil War the monarch, Charles I, is executed.

1863
The world's first underground railway opens in London.

AD 122
Romans build Hadrian's Wall to separate the northern part of Great Britain from the south, which was part of their empire.

c. AD 397
Scotland's first Christian church, in Whithorn, is set up by St Ninian.

AD 685
The Picts win the Battle of Dun Nechtain, keeping the Northumbrian king out of what we now call Scotland.

1314
An army led by Robert the Bruce defeats the English at the Battle of Bannockburn.

1328
At the Treaty of Northampton, England recognises Scotland as an independent country, with Robert the Bruce as King of Scotland.

Scotland

Scotland forms the northern part of Great Britain. It is best known for the mountainous Highlands and Islands, and its capital is the city of Edinburgh.

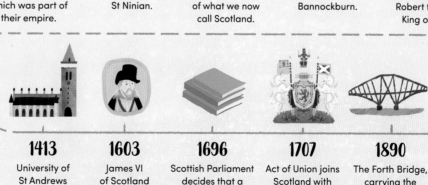
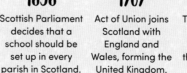

1413
University of St Andrews is established.

1603
James VI of Scotland becomes James I of England.

1696
Scottish Parliament decides that a school should be set up in every parish in Scotland.

1707
Act of Union joins Scotland with England and Wales, forming the United Kingdom.

1890
The Forth Bridge, carrying the railway across the Firth of Forth, is built.

1999
The new Scottish Parliament sits in Edinburgh.

AD 48
The Romans invade Wales, but are slowed down by resistance led by Caradog (Caratacus).

AD 550
St David founds a monastery, which becomes a major shrine for Christians.

c. AD 780–790
King Offa builds a huge earth barrier (dyke) to separate his kingdom, Mercia, from Wales.

1067 onwards
The Normans gradually gain control over much of Wales, despite strong resistance.

1284
Edward I of England conquers most of Wales and builds strong castles.

Wales
Wales is the smallest of the nations that form Great Britain. Its capital and largest city is Cardiff. The flag of Wales features a red dragon, which is considered a symbol of power.

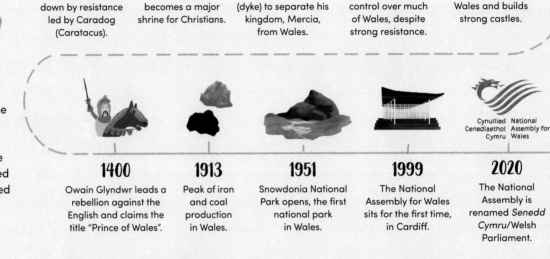

Cynulliad Cenedlaethol Cymru
National Assembly for Wales

1400
Owain Glyndwr leads a rebellion against the English and claims the title "Prince of Wales".

1913
Peak of iron and coal production in Wales.

1951
Snowdonia National Park opens, the first national park in Wales.

1999
The National Assembly for Wales sits for the first time, in Cardiff.

2020
The National Assembly is renamed *Senedd Cymru*/Welsh Parliament.

AD 432
St Patrick travels from Armagh throughout Ireland to spread Christianity.

1169
The Normans land in Ireland at the request of Dermot MacMurrough, the former King of Leinster.

1609
James I gives land in Ulster to English and Scottish settlers, as part of the Plantation of Ulster.

1690
William III defeats the supporters of ousted James II at the Battle of the Boyne.

1801
Act of Union makes the whole island of Ireland part of the United Kingdom.

Northern Ireland
Northern Ireland is the smallest part of the UK, and the only part that is not in Great Britain. Its capital, Belfast, is one of the UK's largest cities and is home to about one-third of Northern Ireland's population.

1829
After a long campaign led by Daniel O'Connell, Catholic Emancipation is granted. Catholics are now allowed to sit in the Westminster parliament.

1845–1849
The Great Famine, a time of hardship and hunger, leads to the deaths of more than one million people.

1921
Northern Ireland is established and Ireland is partitioned.

1969
The Troubles – a conflict that went on for almost 30 years – begin.

1998
The Belfast (Good Friday) Agreement signals an end to the Troubles. The Northern Ireland Assembly sits for the first time, at Stormont.

"Your map was so helpful," exclaimed Isabella as she settled down in Great Granny's comfy armchair. "I understand how the four nations fit together now. So, The Queen reigns over the UK today, but who ruled these four nations in the past?"

"Good question!" smiled Great Granny Joyce, putting her arm around Isabella. "Let me tell you about some of them..."

Hywel Dda
Reigned AD 910–927

Hywel's name means "Hywel the Good" in Welsh. Under his rule, most of Wales was united in a kingdom called Deheubarth. After he established peace, Hywel brought in laws that focused on fairness and justice, and these formed the basis of Welsh life for centuries.

Athelstan
Reigned AD 925–939

After Alfred the Great defeated the Vikings, his grandson Athelstan united the country and became the first king of all England. During his reign, England was at peace. He built many churches and monasteries, and was famous throughout Europe as a wise and fair king.

Brian Boru
Reigned 1002–1014

Brian was king of a province called Munster. He then conquered Leinster, another province, and defeated the Vikings. According to legend, Brian refused to fight and kill people on holy days, such as Good Friday. His harp is still regarded as the symbol of the Republic of Ireland.

Macbeth
Reigned 1040–1057

Macbeth seized the throne of Scotland in 1040 after killing Duncan I in battle. He was an effective ruler. He changed the law so daughters and sons had equal inheritance rights. The son of Duncan I attacked Scotland in 1054 and killed Macbeth in battle in 1057.

Amazing! Every nation has so much history...

Mary, Queen of Scots
Reigned 1542–1567

Mary's reign over Scotland proved difficult and she was forced off the throne in 1567. She fled to England, but was captured and kept in prison by Elizabeth I for many years. Later, in 1587, Mary was executed after being accused of helping an attempt to overthrow Elizabeth I.

Great Granny Joyce turned to face Isabella.

"The great thing about having lots of different monarchs and separate histories of the UK nations is that we now have many different cultures."

"Wow! How can I find out more about all the different parts?"

"Here!" said Great Granny Joyce, handing over a leaflet from the Treasures Box. "You can read about all the remarkable things our country has to offer."

Sports

The UK is the birthplace of many sports, including football, tennis, cricket, golf, and rugby. Other traditional sports are also enjoyed, such as Gaelic football, hurling, cnapan (similar to rugby), and shinty (similar to hockey). London is the only city to have hosted the Olympic Games three times, while Edinburgh has hosted the Commonwealth Games twice. Rugby is played at the Principality Stadium in Cardiff, Gaelic games at Casement Park in Belfast, and Highland Games events are held across Scotland. In England, there is tennis at Wimbledon and football finals at Wembley Stadium.

Cricket

Football

Gaelic football

Welsh Red Dragon

Snowdon / Yr Wyddfa, Wales

Look at these beautiful lochs and mountains! I'd love to go on a trip around the UK, Great Granny Joyce!

Languages

As well as English, the UK has 10 other native languages, including Scottish Gaelic and Irish Gaelic, Scots, Ulster-Scots, Cornish, and Welsh. Wales is bilingual, which means both English and Welsh have official status. More than 500,000 people speak Welsh. Some children speak Welsh at home and others learn it in school. Welsh is written on road signs, in shops, and on public buildings. There is a Welsh-language television channel, Welsh bands that play all kinds of music, and a huge variety of Welsh-language books to read and enjoy.

Loch Ness, Scotland

Landscape and culture

The UK has a varied landscape, from the rolling hills and valleys of Wales to Scottish glens and moorlands, and from the rugged coastline of Northern Ireland to England's lush farmland. World Heritage Sites include Stonehenge in England, Edinburgh's Old and New Towns in Scotland, Pontcysyllte Aqueduct and Canal in Wales, and the Giant's Causeway in Northern Ireland. Each nation has its own cultural associations. You might think of afternoon tea and cricket in England, haggis and tartan in Scotland, Welsh cakes and daffodils in Wales, and soda bread and folk music in Northern Ireland, but this is just a tiny part of the UK's truly diverse cultures and traditions.

Edinburgh Castle, Scotland

Giant's Causeway, Northern Ireland

Bodhrán (Irish drum)

Red telephone box

Irish flute

The arts

The UK has excelled in literature and drama, from the historic plays of William Shakespeare to the more recent works of authors Kate Roberts, Julia Donaldson, and Malorie Blackman. Outstanding film and television performances include those by actors John Boyega, Michelle Fairley, and Ewan McGregor. Festivals, such as eisteddfods in Wales, showcase poetic and musical talents. The Queen has seen many UK singers and musicians emerge during her reign. At the annual Royal Variety Performance, The Queen has enjoyed performances by Tom Jones, Susan Boyle, Ed Sheeran, and Emeli Sandé.

John Boyega

Emeli Sandé

Tom Jones

Michelle Fairley

Isabella had learned so much about the UK, and she couldn't wait to hear more. While Great Granny Joyce was busy in the kitchen, Isabella made another discovery.

A large piece of paper was curled up at the very bottom of the Treasures Box. Isabella unrolled it and, using anything she could find to hold it down, spread it out on the floor. It was a map of the world! Isabella loved looking at maps and having the world laid out before her.

At that moment, Great Granny Joyce walked in and her eyes widened when she saw the map.

"Oh! The world map! Now that's another story..."

Isabella picked up the map and sat with her great granny on the armchair. Great Granny's old ginger cat, Tiger, tried to sneak a peek, too.

Isabella was keen to show Great Granny Joyce what she had learned at school, so she began pointing out the continents: "Europe... where we live, Africa, Asia, Oceania, North America, South America, and Antarctica."

"That's right!" said Great Granny Joyce. "I love to travel and see the world. I'm a bit like The Queen really. Her Majesty has been to many places. So many more than me! Her first overseas trip was a visit to southern Africa when she was 20. Since then, she has seen the elephants in India, admired the Sydney Harbour Bridge in Australia, and so much more. In fact, she's visited almost every country in the Commonwealth!"

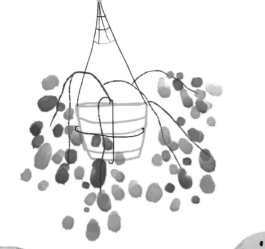

Isabella wondered about this latest mysterious word. "What is the Commonwealth? I've never heard of it."

Great Granny Joyce replied, "The Commonwealth is a group of countries that work together. The Queen is Head of the Commonwealth. She has been to many meetings of the government leaders, and every March, on Commonwealth Day, she sends a message to all Commonwealth citizens."

What does the Commonwealth do?

Today, the Commonwealth is an equal group of countries. Its roots go back to the 16th Century, when Britain began to expand its Empire. During the 20th Century, countries that had been part of the British Empire started to gain independence. Many came together to form the Commonwealth. In 1949, all Commonwealth members were recognised as independent and equal to one another and it was decided that other countries could be part of the Commonwealth. The modern Commonwealth of nations was born. This aims for a fairer future for its citizens by promoting peace, improving education and healthcare, helping poorer countries, and by addressing global problems such as climate change. Each country has an equal voice. In 2018, The Prince of Wales was chosen to be the next Head of the Commonwealth.

The Commonwealth countries

This map shows the countries of the Commonwealth today. Membership of the modern Commonwealth is not dependent on having any historical connections to Britain. Since its creation, membership has grown to 54 countries, spread all around the world. At the start, the only members were Australia, Canada, New Zealand, and South Africa.

Canada

> Like many people from the Commonwealth, I came to the UK during the 1950s, around the start of The Queen's reign.

Jamaica
Joined in 1962

Jamaica is the third-largest island in the Caribbean, known for its white sandy beaches, crystal clear waters, dense rainforests, and towering mountains.

The Bahamas

Belize

St Kitts and Nevis

Antigua and Barbuda
Dominica
Saint Lucia
Barbados
St Vincent and the Grenadines

Grenada

Guyana

Trinidad and Tobago
Joined in 1962

Trinidad and Tobago is the location of Pitch Lake, the largest natural deposit of asphalt in the world, which replenishes itself despite being emptied again and again to pave roads.

Commonwealth immigration

Immigration means coming to one country from another and making a new home there. After World War II, there were lots of job vacancies in the UK, so the government offered all Commonwealth citizens free entry into the UK. Some employers paid the fares for people to come to work in the National Health Service (NHS), in factories, and on railways. The first people to arrive came from the Caribbean. They are often known as the "Windrush Generation", after *Empire Windrush*, a ship that brought 500 people to the UK in 1948. It wasn't easy to move so far from home, and many people also faced discrimination (unfair treatment) at work and in their neighbourhoods. During the 1960s, most of the Commonwealth citizens who immigrated to the UK were from India and Pakistan.

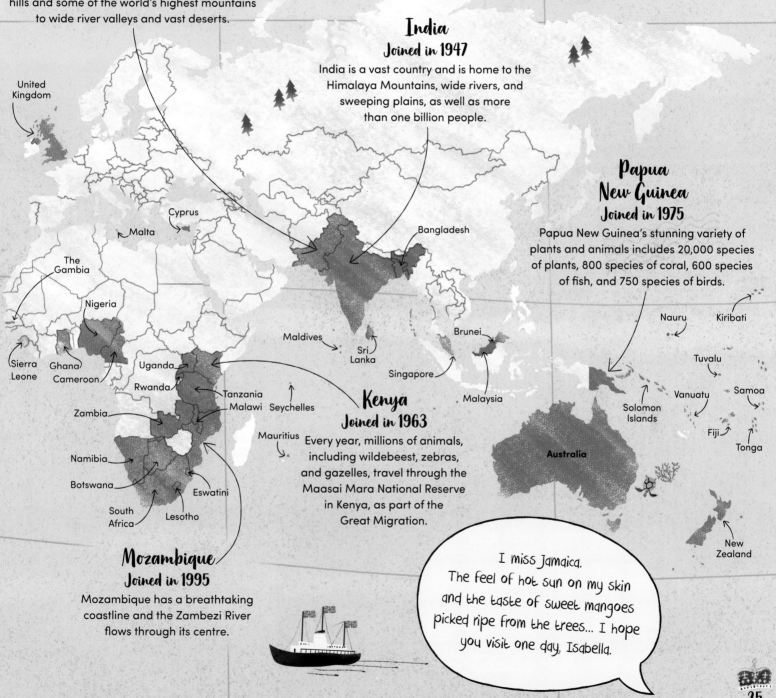

Key

Commonwealth countries

Pakistan
Joined in 1947, left in 1972, rejoined in 1989

Pakistan has a rich landscape, from forested hills and some of the world's highest mountains to wide river valleys and vast deserts.

India
Joined in 1947

India is a vast country and is home to the Himalaya Mountains, wide rivers, and sweeping plains, as well as more than one billion people.

Papua New Guinea
Joined in 1975

Papua New Guinea's stunning variety of plants and animals includes 20,000 species of plants, 800 species of coral, 600 species of fish, and 750 species of birds.

Kenya
Joined in 1963

Every year, millions of animals, including wildebeest, zebras, and gazelles, travel through the Maasai Mara National Reserve in Kenya, as part of the Great Migration.

Mozambique
Joined in 1995

Mozambique has a breathtaking coastline and the Zambezi River flows through its centre.

United Kingdom

Cyprus

Malta

The Gambia

Nigeria

Sierra Leone

Ghana

Cameroon

Uganda

Rwanda

Zambia

Tanzania

Malawi

Seychelles

Mauritius

Namibia

Botswana

Eswatini

South Africa

Lesotho

Maldives

Sri Lanka

Bangladesh

Brunei

Singapore

Malaysia

Nauru

Kiribati

Tuvalu

Vanuatu

Samoa

Solomon Islands

Fiji

Tonga

Australia

New Zealand

I miss Jamaica. The feel of hot sun on my skin and the taste of sweet mangoes picked ripe from the trees... I hope you visit one day, Isabella.

Commonwealth campaigners

The 54 countries of the Commonwealth are home to about 2.5 billion people. Many people from these nations have changed the world for the better by campaigning for causes they believed in or fighting against injustice. Here are just a few Commonwealth campaigners who have left an unforgettable legacy.

Ngozi Okonjo-Iweala

In 2021, Nigerian–American economist Ngozi Okonjo-Iweala (b. 1954) became the seventh Director-General of the World Trade Organisation (WTO), which ensures that global trade takes place fairly. She is the first woman and the first African to hold this role.

Learie Constantine

A world-class cricketer from Trinidad and Tobago, Learie Constantine (1901–1971) was also a lawyer, politician, and campaigner against racial discrimination. He was made a baron and became the first black person to take his seat in the UK's House of Lords.

Wangari Maathai

Kenyan environmentalist and activist Wangari Maathai (1940–2011) founded the Green Belt Movement in 1977, which led to the planting of more than 50 million trees in Kenya. In 2004, she became the first African woman to win the Nobel Peace Prize.

Benazir Bhutto

Pakistani Benazir Bhutto (1953–2007) was the first woman in her country to become Prime Minister when she took charge in 1988. She was also the first Muslim woman ever to become a head of government. She served as Prime Minister twice for a total period of five years.

Nelson Mandela

South African lawyer Nelson Mandela (1918–2013) led efforts to end apartheid, and spent 27 years in prison for going against the racist government. After his release, Mandela became the first president of the newly democratic South Africa. He went on to win the Nobel Peace Prize, as well as more than 250 other awards.

Malala Yousafzai

Pakistani schoolgirl and activist Malala Yousafzai (b. 1997) stood up against the Taliban, a religious military group, by demanding that girls be allowed to attend school. She survived being shot by the Taliban, and then went on to graduate from Oxford University. In 2014, she became the youngest person ever to win the Nobel Peace Prize.

Chapter Two
Family and Friends

What a day of learning! From coronations to the Commonwealth, it was all new to Isabella. She turned back to the Treasures Box and pulled out some paper covered with photographs of people.

"Look at our family tree!" said Great Granny Joyce in delight.

Isabella ran over to the window, but all she found was a giant oak outside. "Hmmm, it's an impressive tree, but it's not really part of our family."

Great Granny Joyce giggled at her great granddaughter.
"Not that tree! The family tree, on that paper you're holding!"

"Oh!" laughed Isabella, looking more closely. "Look, that's me right there!"

"Of course, you're one of the most recent additions to our family. There's your brother and sister, your mum and dad, your granny and grandad, and then there's me and your Great Grandad Winston!"

"And there's your mum and dad at the top!"

"I do miss them," sighed Great Granny. "It's lovely to look back at photographs and remember the happy times we all shared."

Just look how glamorous I was back then!

Great Great Granny Olga

1905–1990

Great Grandad Winston
1925–2008

Grandad Tony

b. 1948

Dad (Nathan)

b. 1976

Amelia

b. 2008

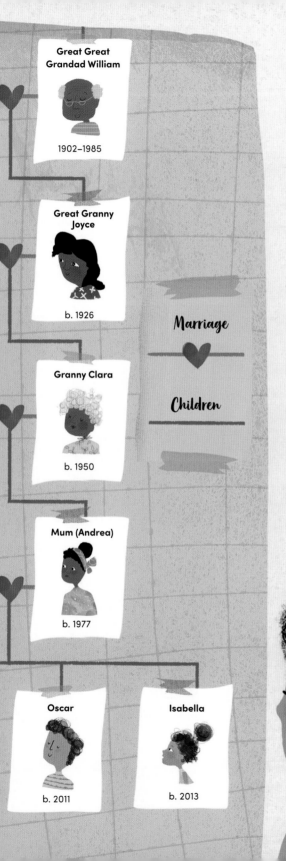

Great Great Grandad William

1902–1985

Great Granny Joyce

b. 1926

Marriage

Children

Granny Clara

b. 1950

Mum (Andrea)

b. 1977

Oscar

b. 2011

Isabella

b. 2013

"Does our family tree go back further?" asked Isabella.

"Yes, it does. You're just the latest in a long line of our family. Isn't that an exciting thought?"

Isabella studied her family tree for a long time, taking it all in. Finally, she asked a question.

"Does The Queen have a family tree?"

"She does indeed. One of the most famous families is the Royal Family. I have a copy of their family tree in my Treasures Box, too. Now where is it?"

Isabella gazed at her Great Granny Joyce in wonder as she stuck her head inside the box and started rummaging.

"Here it is!" Great Granny Joyce pulled out the Royal Family tree and unfolded it for Isabella to see...

You look so much like your mum – and I look just like mine!

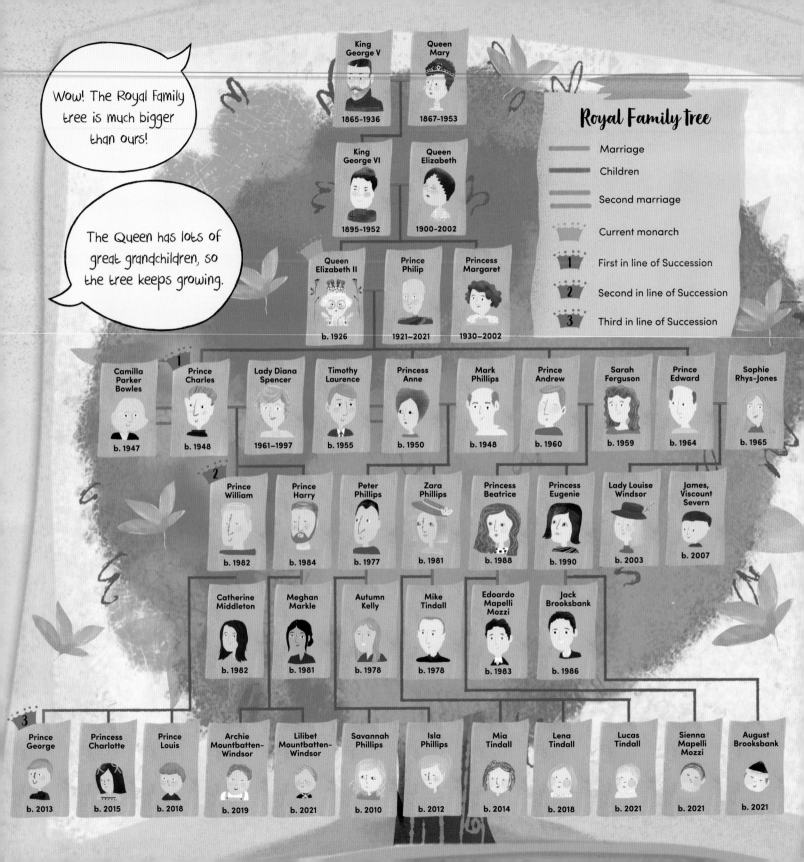

David I of Scotland
Reigned 1124–1153

David I made Scotland a united country, turning towns such as Berwick and Edinburgh into centres of trade. He encouraged learning, and founded many monasteries. Many people at the time called him a saint.

Henry VIII of England
Reigned 1509–1547

Crowned king aged 18, Henry ruled for 38 years. When he divorced his first wife, his quarrel with the Roman Catholic Church led to the creation of the Church of England. He married six times, divorcing two of his wives and executing two: Anne Boleyn and Catherine Howard.

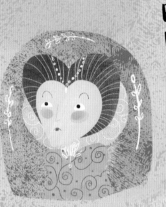

Elizabeth I of England
Reigned 1558–1603

Elizabeth I was the daughter of Henry VIII and Anne Boleyn. She ruled for almost 45 years and during her reign, England's power in the world increased. The strong English navy defeated the Spanish Armada, and explorer Sir Francis Drake became the first English person to sail around the world.

Queen Victoria
Reigned 1837–1901

Queen Victoria's reign lasted almost 64 years. This was a time of great progress in technology and industry, and the UK became very powerful, ruling many other countries. These countries were known as the British Empire. By 1900, Queen Victoria was Empress of about a quarter of the world's population.

The House of Windsor

The Royal Family of the United Kingdom is called the House of Windsor. During World War I, when the UK was fighting Germany, King George V decided to change his German surname Saxe-Coburg-Gotha to Windsor. This marked the start of the House of Windsor. King George V was the grandson of Queen Victoria and the grandfather of Queen Elizabeth II. All the Members of the Royal Family today are descended from King George V and his wife, Queen Mary.

I recognise these kings and queens from my history lessons at school!

After looking at the Royal Family tree, Isabella's jaw dropped open. "The Queen certainly has a big family."

"It gets even bigger if you include The Queen's many, many pets!" laughed Great Granny Joyce.

"Oh, of course! How could I forget!" chuckled Isabella.

Royal horses

Queen Elizabeth II began horse riding as a little girl. Her Majesty has owned about 100 horses and personally chooses all their names. About 20 of them became successful racehorses. The Queen also loves to watch horse racing, and goes to the Royal Ascot race meeting most years.

"I think for my birthday this year, I'm going to ask for a dog! I would really love a pet."

"Did you know that The Queen was given a Shetland pony for her fourth birthday? Her name was Peggy! This inspired The Queen to take up horse riding and, later, she started owning racehorses."

Inside the Treasures Box, Isabella came across some old newspaper cuttings showing The Queen's love of horses.

"I don't think I could ever get a pony," giggled Isabella. "It would never fit in our garden!"

Furry friends

The Queen has always adored corgis. The word "corgi" means dwarf dog in Welsh, and the breed was once used by farmers to herd cattle. In 1933, when The Queen was a young princess, her father brought home a corgi named Dookie. Princess Elizabeth enjoyed looking after Dookie and her love of corgis began. The Queen has owned about 30 corgis. Almost all of them were descended from Susan, a corgi that was given to Princess Elizabeth on her 18th birthday. The Queen has also owned cocker spaniels and dorgis – a cross between a dachshund and a corgi.

Isabella pulled up a stool so she could rummage inside the Treasures Box. Every time she moved one treasure it revealed another, just as exciting as the one before. Then Isabella paused and looked up at her great granny.

"What makes the Royal Family, the Royal Family? Why can't we also be the Royal Family?" asked Isabella curiously.

"That's a great question," replied Great Granny Joyce. "There is a long line of rulers in their family. The right to rule is passed down to family members. More than 1,000 years ago, Athelstan was the first monarch to rule England. Queen Elizabeth II can trace her family back to him! There were kings and queens in Ireland, Scotland, and Wales, too."

"I'm a bit confused by so many monarchs," Isabella said.

"Wait a minute, I've got a book somewhere that explains it all," said Great Granny Joyce. She took a book off the shelf and handed it to Isabella.

After she had finished reading about the British monarchy, Isabella asked, "So if the government is in charge of running the country, what does The Queen do?"

Monarchy

In the past, many countries were led by a king, a queen, or an emperor called a monarch. Monarchs had all the power to make laws for the people of their countries. Some democratic countries, including the UK, now have a constitutional monarchy, which means there is both a monarch and an elected government. The government is responsible for making the laws and decisions on behalf of everyone. As well as working with the government, The Queen serves the country and Commonwealth by encouraging unity, recognising individual achievements, and serving as a stable and unifying presence in all our lives.

Parliamentary duties

The Queen carries out these official duties at the UK Parliament based in London, as well as others in those of Scotland, Wales, and Northern Ireland.

- When Members of Parliament pass a new law, The Queen must approve it for it to become valid. This is also known as giving Royal Assent.

- In order for the UK Parliament to resume after a break, The Queen must open it. This usually happens once a year (known as the State Opening of Parliament), but always after a general election.

- When a general election has been won by a political party, The Queen asks the leader of the party to become Prime Minister, and to create a new government in her name.

- The Queen gives advice to the Prime Minister at their weekly meetings.

Great Granny Joyce explained The Queen's parliamentary duties to Isabella.

"That sounds like a very big to-do list!" said Isabella.

"And The Queen has many other duties to fit in, too. Her Majesty is kept very busy, I can tell you."

"Being The Queen isn't as easy as I first thought!" said Isabella.

"Now, we don't want to overload your brain. Let's take a break and have something to drink."

Great Granny Joyce and Isabella moved to the comfy armchairs to sip their refreshing squash. What a treat!

They sat facing the fireplace, with all the family photographs on the mantelpiece. One was of Great Granny Joyce and Great Grandad Winston on their wedding day.

"I love that picture. You two were married for so long!" smiled Isabella.

Great Granny Joyce smiled back, "I know! Can you believe that The Queen was married for even longer?"

Isabella remembered reading that The Queen was married. "How long?"

Great Granny Joyce passed Isabella a photograph of The Queen and Prince Philip. "73 years! What a couple they made – the future queen and the handsome sailor! They married in 1947, the year before my own wedding. Such a long, happy partnership they had!"

You've read fairy tales about princes and princesses, great love stories that stand the test of time. Love changes people's lives, just like it did for Winston and me.

I love these pictures. I can't believe The Queen was married for 73 years! That's sooooo long!

36

The Queen and Prince Philip

1934
Meet as children

1947
Engaged and married

1948
First son, Charles, is born

1950
Only daughter, Anne, is born

1952
Queen Elizabeth begins her reign

1960
Second son, Andrew, is born

1964
Third son, Edward, is born

1997
Celebrate golden wedding anniversary – 50 years married

2017
Celebrate platinum wedding anniversary – 70 years married

2021
Prince Philip dies aged 99

At 10 o'clock the next morning, Isabella was peeking out of a window at Great Granny's house. She was excited because her cousin Rhys from Wales and two of her school friends were coming over during the half-term holiday. As Isabella spotted them all coming up the drive, she ran to the front door and flung it open.

Great Granny smiled and said, "Come in, come in, you're all very welcome. So good to see you again, Rhys. My, you've grown!"

Rhys laughed as Great Granny Joyce ruffled his hair.

"We're so excited to meet you," one of Isabella's friends said to Great Granny Joyce. "Isabella has been telling our teacher and class all about you."

"I'm excited to meet you, too. Isabella often tells me about you all. Now let me find some treats," replied Great Granny Joyce.

Soon there was squash and fruitcake for everyone. Isabella proudly showed her cousin and her friends the Treasures Box.

"Don't you think this would be perfect to take into school for the special Jubilee Show and Tell?" she asked.

Isabella's friends nodded in agreement, but Great Granny Joyce and Rhys looked at each other in confusion.

"What's Show and Tell?" asked Great Granny Joyce.

"Aha! Now it's my turn to teach you something," giggled Isabella. "At certain times of the year, we bring something special to Show and Tell with our class. We talk about what it is and why it's important. Our next Show and Tell is about the Platinum Jubilee celebrations."

Great Granny Joyce frowned and said, "The Treasures Box is too big though. Why don't you each pick one thing to take in and talk about?"

Isabella's friends chose newspaper cuttings from The Queen's Coronation and a commemorative coin from the 1977 Silver Jubilee.

Isabella picked out some Coronation bunting that Great Granny Joyce had made in 1953 to decorate her home. Although the colours had faded over time, the bunting still looked lovely.

"Thank you, Great Granny Joyce!" they all said together.

This was going to be the best Show and Tell ever!

The following weekend, there was lots of excitement at Isabella's house.
Isabella and her cousin had been so inspired by the souvenirs in the
Treasures Box that the family had decided to go on a tour of London.
Rhys was thrilled – he hadn't been to London before.

Great Granny Joyce didn't join them for their day in the city,
but Isabella and Rhys promised to video call her for the best bits.

Sitting on the top deck of the sightseeing bus, they shrieked with
amazement as each famous landmark came into view.

"There's just so much to see!" Isabella shouted into her phone.
"And I can't wait to see the Tower of London, where they keep
the Crown Jewels. Look, Great Granny! There's Big Ben!"

"Oh yes!" replied Great Granny Joyce. "Big Ben is actually the huge bell that chimes to mark the time. The clock tower that houses Big Ben was named Elizabeth Tower in 2012, in honour of The Queen's Diamond Jubilee. Ha! I can be your virtual tour guide!"

"I never knew that! Oh, where are we now? The Houses of Parliament... Horse Guards Parade... the London Eye... Buckingham Palace!"

The Palace looked stunning in the spring sunshine. A home fit for a queen! The tour guide told them that the royal palace has 775 rooms, as well as a ballroom, chapel, tennis court, swimming pool, and a post office.

Isabella and Rhys repeated this information to Great Granny.

"Just imagine keeping all those rooms clean!" said Great Granny, and they all laughed.

Soon after, they stopped outside Westminster Abbey, where Princess Elizabeth and Prince Philip got married.

The tour guide explained that the wedding was attended by 2,000 guests and that the Princess wore a dress handmade by 350 dressmakers. The guide went on, "Their wedding rings were made of rare Welsh gold. Since then, all royal weddings have featured Welsh gold rings, including the weddings of Prince William and Catherine Middleton in 2011, and Prince Harry and Meghan Markle in 2018."

When the tour was over, Isabella thought, "Maybe I could make my own Treasures Box filled with memories from amazing days like today!"

Residences and retreats

There are residences and retreats all over the UK with a variety of royal connections. Steeped in history and tradition, these special places include castles, palaces, and houses. From formidable fortifications to holiday homes, all have links to the British Royal Family, or to past royal rulers, governors, and chieftains from the four UK nations.

Scotland

9 Edinburgh Castle
Edinburgh

10 Dumfries House
Ayrshire

11 Palace of Holyroodhouse
Edinburgh

12 Glamis Castle
Forfar

13 Balmoral Castle
Aberdeenshire

14 Castle of Mey
Caithness

Northern Ireland

1 Enniskillen Castle Museums
County Fermanagh

2 Hillsborough Castle
County Down

3 Gosford Castle
County Armagh

4 Glenarm Castle
County Antrim

England

15 Sandringham House
Norfolk

16 Buckingham Palace
London

17 Clarence House
London

18 Windsor Castle
Berkshire

19 Osborne House
Isle of Wight

Wales

5 Llwynywermod
Carmarthenshire

6 Pembroke Castle
Pembrokeshire

7 Caernarfon Castle
Caernarfon

8 Monmouth Castle
Monmouthshire

The Succession to the
Crown Act 2013

Chapter Three
Ambitions and Achievements

The next time Isabella visited her great granny, the Treasures Box was out on the living-room floor, waiting for her. She sat down and began combing through the lifetime of treasures.

"What are you doing in this picture? You look like you're wearing a uniform."

Great Granny Joyce was dressed as a nurse in the black-and-white picture.

"I worked in a hospital after World War II. I was very young, but there was a shortage of nurses. We all had to step up and do our part."

"I never knew that! I'm so proud of you." Isabella was amazed at all the things she was finding out about Great Granny Joyce.

"Thank you, but I was just one of many. The Queen stepped up in troubled times, too. On her 21st birthday, in 1947, Princess Elizabeth made a radio speech dedicating her life to the service of the Commonwealth."

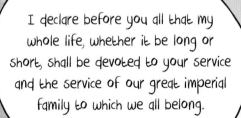

You became a nurse when times were tough, Great Granny. Just like Princess Elizabeth became Queen in sad circumstances. It's very inspiring!

Isabella was impressed.

"When she was only 25, Princess Elizabeth's father, King George VI, died suddenly," Great Granny Joyce continued. "The Princess was in Kenya at the time, on a royal tour. Not only was it devastating to hear about the death of her father, but The Princess was next in line to the throne. It was now her responsibility to lead the country. She was so brave and resilient."

"What an incredible woman!" exclaimed Isabella.

"You can say that again. We can all learn a thing or two from our Queen."

Isabella was learning about World War II at school. On a trip to the local museum, she and her classmates were each given a replica wartime ration book to keep. During the war some foods, such as sugar and meat, were very scarce. Ration books set out what people could buy each week, so that everything was shared out fairly.

Isabella leafed through the pages of the book.

"What was it like during the war?" she asked. "Did you have a ration book like this, too?"

"Well, I was a teenager in Jamaica at the time. My father was away, serving in the British army," Great Granny Joyce said. "Life was tough. We didn't have ration books like people did in the UK, but things like petrol, sugar, and flour were hard to find. Your other Great Granny Margaret lived in Liverpool during the Blitz. She and her family had to hide in shelters while bombs dropped overhead. It must have been terrifying! With food rationing, there were no extra slices of fruitcake either. In fact, there was rarely cake at all."

"That sounds terrible, Great Granny Joyce. What was the Blitz?"

Great Granny passed Isabella a newspaper article from the Treasures Box.

The Blitz

During World War II, from September 1940 to May 1941, Nazi planes continually bombed several cities in the UK, and about 40,000 people were killed. This bombing campaign became known as the Blitz.

Wartime service

Princess Elizabeth played an important role in the Auxiliary Territorial Service, the women's branch of the British Army during World War II. She was the first woman in the Royal Family to become an active-duty member of the British Armed Forces. She got her hands dirty as a mechanic, and also passed the military driving test to work as a driver.

"Sounds really scary," Isabella frowned as she was reading.

"It was, but everyone just had to keep calm and carry on! And guess who showed us all how to cope in wartime?" Great Granny Joyce asked, while hiding a picture behind her back.

"The Queen!" Isabella knew her great granny's heroine by now.

"Yes!" declared Great Granny Joyce, pulling out a photograph of Princess Elizabeth as a girl. "This picture was taken during World War II. Although she was so young, she stayed strong. She did a radio show called *Children's Hour* to cheer children up and lift their spirits.

"Her experience of the war must have helped The Princess prepare for her new role as queen. She has certainly shown the same leadership and courage during her reign as she did during the war. The Queen has seen us through many difficult times with so much strength and hope!"

Isabella beamed at her great granny. She was glad she had so many remarkable women to look up to.

Isabella popped a tamarind ball into her mouth. "This is yummy! Where did you learn to make food like this, Great Granny Joyce?"

"At school in Jamaica. Back then, classes were divided so girls were taught to cook, while boys did woodwork. And it wasn't just in Jamaica, it was the same for your Great Granny Margaret too, here in the UK!"

"So Rhys and I would have been in different classes? That doesn't seem right." Isabella wrinkled her nose in disapproval. "All children should be able to do the same subjects."

Great Granny nodded, "I agree. But things have changed a lot since then. Over the years, people have fought hard to bring about equality.

Now boys and girls can study whatever subjects they want. In the past, women weren't allowed to vote either."

"What do you mean?" asked Isabella.

Great Granny continued, "For a very long time, only men were allowed to vote in elections. But campaigners made sure this all changed so every adult could vote to keep things fair and equal. Now, when you turn 18, you can vote, too. And for the Scottish Parliament, Welsh Parliament, and local elections, young people can vote at the age of 16. There have been changes within the Royal Family, too. Now, whoever is the first-born child of the monarch is the future ruler. The sons of a monarch are no longer given priority."

Great Granny Joyce flicked through the souvenirs in her Treasures Box. "Here it is!" She handed Isabella a newspaper article about the change in the law.

"That's more like it!" smiled Isabella when she had finished reading.

"Yes, and it was The Queen who championed the Act all the way through. The Queen became the monarch because she was the eldest of two daughters and there were no sons. But she made sure there were equal opportunities for all her family members in the future, regardless of whether they were boys or girls."

"Yay! So much has happened even in my lifetime!" said Isabella.

"And you've only heard a bit of it!" replied Great Granny Joyce. "There's plenty more where that came from..."

The Succession to the Crown Act 2013

In the past, the monarchy gave preferential treatment to princes over princesses. This meant the first son of a monarch would become heir to the throne, instead of his elder sister. In 2013, the UK Parliament passed the Succession to the Crown Act to stop this inequality. Now, the eldest child, whether a boy or a girl, will take the throne. As The Queen's eldest child, Prince Charles is first in line to the throne. His eldest child, Prince William, is second in line to the throne.

The Prince of Wales will be the next monarch because he is The Queen's eldest child.

In Her Majesty's lifetime

VOTES FOR WOMEN

1926
Elizabeth's birth
Princess Elizabeth is born, the eldest daughter of the future King George VI and Queen Elizabeth.

1928
Right to vote
Following years of campaigning, voting rights are given to all women aged 21 and over in the UK.

1936
Crowned king
Princess Elizabeth's father is crowned King George VI after the abdication of his brother King Edward VIII.

1939
World War II
World War II begins and becomes the biggest war in history. More than 30 countries take part.

1948
Free healthcare
England, Wales, and Scotland launch the NHS (National Health Service), and Northern Ireland introduces the HSC (Health and Social Care) service to provide free healthcare for all.

1949
The modern Commonwealth
The Commonwealth countries meet and agree that all the nations in the Commonwealth are equal and independent.

1952
Queen Elizabeth II
Queen Elizabeth becomes Queen of the UK and Head of the Commonwealth, following the death of her father, King George VI.

May 1953
Mount Everest
New Zealander Edmund Hillary and Sherpa Tenzing Norgay are the first to climb Mount Everest, the world's tallest mountain, just before Coronation Day.

June 1953
The Queen's Coronation
Elizabeth is officially crowned Queen in a grand ceremony at Westminster Abbey.

I can't believe all this has happened since The Queen was born!

2000
Millennium celebrations
New Year celebrations around the world mark the beginning of the 21st century.

2002
Royal funeral
The Queen Mother (the mother of The Queen) dies peacefully, aged 101.

2011
William's wedding
Prince William marries Catherine Middleton at Westminster Abbey. They become The Duke and Duchess of Cambridge.

2012
London Olympics
London hosts the Olympic Games for a record-breaking third time. The previous times London hosted the Games were 1908 and 1948.

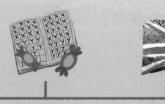

1940
Rationing begins

Rationing is introduced so that limited food and fuel supplies can be shared out fairly during wartime.

8 May 1945
VE Day

Germany surrenders, ending World War II in Europe. Celebrations mark VE (Victory in Europe) Day.

15 August 1945
VJ Day

Japan surrenders, making VJ (Victory over Japan) Day the official end of World War II.

October 1945
United Nations

The United Nations (UN) is formed after World War II for nations to come together to debate and discuss, while avoiding conflict.

1947
Elizabeth & Philip

Princess Elizabeth marries Philip Mountbatten at Westminster Abbey. They go on to have four children: Charles, Anne, Andrew, and Edward.

1 July 1969
Prince of Wales

A ceremony at Caernarfon Castle recognises The Queen's eldest son, Charles, as His Royal Highness The Prince of Wales.

24 July 1969
Moon landing

On the Apollo 11 space mission, US astronauts Neil Armstrong and Buzz Aldrin become the first people to set foot on the Moon.

1979
A first for women

Margaret Thatcher becomes the first woman to be the Prime Minister of the UK.

1981
Royal wedding

The Prince of Wales marries Lady Diana Spencer at St Paul's Cathedral.

1982
Mary Rose raised

Henry VIII's warship, *Mary Rose*, is raised from the seabed near Portsmouth, where it had sunk during a battle in 1545.

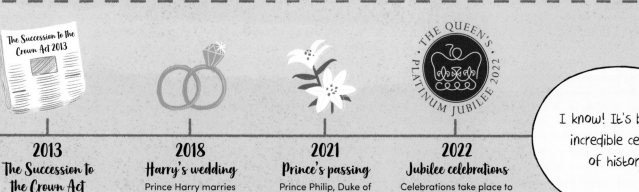

2013
The Succession to the Crown Act

A new law is passed, stating that the eldest child of the monarch automatically becomes heir to the throne.

2018
Harry's wedding

Prince Harry marries Meghan Markle at Windsor Castle. They become The Duke and Duchess of Sussex.

2021
Prince's passing

Prince Philip, Duke of Edinburgh, The Queen's husband for 73 years, dies aged 99.

2022
Jubilee celebrations

Celebrations take place to mark Queen Elizabeth II's 70-year reign.

I know! It's been an incredible century of history!

Isabella was snuggled up on the sofa, stroking furry, purry Tiger.

"So, has anyone ruled our country for longer than The Queen?"

Great Granny Joyce searched through the Treasures Box
and pulled out a magazine article about The Queen.
She read it aloud: "In 2015, Her Majesty became
our nation's longest reigning monarch in history."

"Even longer than Queen Victoria?" asked
Isabella in amazement. She had studied
the Victorians at school last year.

The Queen's Jubilee years

1977
Silver Jubilee
25 years' reign

2002
Golden Jubilee
50 years' reign

2012
Diamond Jubilee
60 years' reign

2017
Sapphire Jubilee
65 years' reign

2022
Platinum Jubilee
70 years' reign

"Even longer than Queen Victoria, who was the great great grandmother of Queen Elizabeth II, by the way. The Queen passed Queen Victoria's record reign of 64 years in 2015. Now The Queen has ruled for 70 years. That's what I call service."

Isabella grabbed some decorations from the Treasures Box. Great Granny Joyce chuckled and joined in.

Did you know that about 140 composers have used the tune of the National Anthem in their music?

God save our gracious Queen,
Long live our noble Queen,
God save The Queen!

National Anthem

The National Anthem was first publicly performed in London in the 18th century, although nobody knows for sure who wrote the music and words. The first version was entitled "God Save The King", as George II was monarch at the time. Now the word "King" has been replaced by "Queen" and usually only the first verse is sung at royal events.

God Save the Queen

God save our gracious Queen,
Long live our noble Queen,
God save The Queen!
Send her victorious,
Happy and glorious,
Long to reign over us,
God save The Queen!

O Lord our God arise,
Scatter our enemies,
And make them fall!
Confound their politics,
Frustrate their knavish tricks,
On Thee our hopes we fix,
God save us all!

Not in this land alone,
But be God's mercies known,
From shore to shore!
Lord make the nations see,
That men should brothers be,
And form one family,
The wide world o'er.

From every latent foe,
From the assassins blow,
God save The Queen!
O'er her thine arm extend,
For Britain's sake defend,
Our mother, prince, and friend,
God save The Queen!

Thy choicest gifts in store,
On her be pleased to pour,
Long may she reign!
May she defend our laws,
And ever give us cause,
To sing with heart and voice,
God save The Queen!

Chapter Four

Charity and Care

"Guess what happened at school this week?" Isabella asked excitedly as she sat down next to Great Granny Joyce.

"Tell me what happened!" Great Granny's eyes twinkled in anticipation.

"The Guide Dogs people came for a visit – with two adorable golden retriever puppies in training. We got to play with them all afternoon. They were so soft and sweet!"

"How wonderful!" Great Granny Joyce smiled. "Guide dogs do such an amazing job supporting blind and partially sighted people."

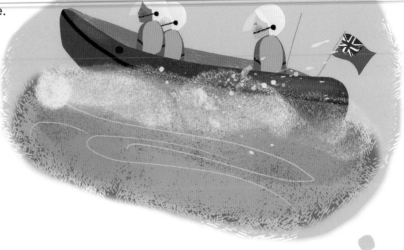

"The school is making a donation to the charity to thank them for coming," exclaimed Isabella.

"That's brilliant! I've always admired the work of the Royal National Lifeboat Institution, saving lives at sea, so I've given them a regular donation for many years now."

"Wait a second," Great Granny Joyce was up again and looking inside the Treasures Box. "Have a look at this..."

The recent newspaper article detailed the huge support The Queen gives to different charities.

"It says here that The Queen is a patron. What is that?" asked Isabella, after she had read the article.

"It's someone who lends their name to support a charity, helping that charity to raise money."

Isabella considered this for a moment. "I'd like to support a charity! Seeing all the doctors and nurses helping poorly people during the COVID-19 pandemic has made me realise how important it is to help others. But how do you choose which charity to support?"

"Pick the charity that you care about the most. If each person picked one charity to help, there would be billions of people making a difference," Great Granny Joyce said.

"Good idea. I'll do some research to help me make up my mind."

Royal fundraiser

The Charities Aid Foundation (CAF) shows that The Queen is among the world's biggest charity supporters, helping charities raise more than £1.4 billion. The Queen is patron of more than 500 British charities, while the Royal Family as a whole supports about 2,500 charities in the UK and another 500 charities across the Commonwealth and worldwide.

Personal donations

The Queen makes her own personal donations to support countries during times of crisis. Among the many people Her Majesty has helped over the years were the victims of devastating earthquakes in Nepal in 2015 and in Italy in 2016.

> "They shall grow not old,
>   as we that are left grow old:
>
> Age shall not weary them,
>   nor the years condemn.
>
> At the going down of the sun
>   and in the morning
>
> We will remember them."

From "For the Fallen"
by Laurence Binyon, 1914

At school, we wear poppies and have a two-minute silence to remember the people who served and died in wars.

Remembrance Sunday

A tradition that is especially important to The Queen is Remembrance Sunday, sometimes called Poppy Day. Many people give money to the Royal British Legion, a British charity that helps war veterans and their families. Red poppies are worn to honour those who fought for their country and lost their lives.

The Prince's Trust

The Prince's Trust was set up by The Prince of Wales in 1976 to support young people aged 11 to 30 who are either facing difficulties at school or unemployment. An annual awards ceremony is held to honour young people who have faced these hardships and worked through them. By 2019, more than one million young people had benefited from the support of the Trust, setting up their own businesses or receiving skills training.

Prince's Trust

> I've heard you can do some really fun things for The Duke of Edinburgh's Award at secondary school, Isabella!

ROYAL FOUNDATION
OF THE DUKE AND DUCHESS OF CAMBRIDGE

The Royal Foundation

The Royal Foundation of The Duke and Duchess of Cambridge is involved with a range of important issues, including climate change, conservation, school support, and mental health. As younger working Members of the Royal Family, the Duke and Duchess are focusing on the issues that matter most to them by investing in the future of our planet.

Future patrons

In 2016, The Queen passed down 25 charity patronages to other Members of the Royal Family in order to ensure her good work continues. The Prince of Wales and The Duchess of Cornwall and The Duke and Duchess of Cambridge have taken over many of these patronages. In 1956, Prince Philip, The Duke of Edinburgh, set up The Duke of Edinburgh's Award to recognise young people for their achievements. Following his death in 2021, Prince Philip's legacy will continue in the 144 countries that run this scheme.

"I still can't pick a charity. I just don't know which to choose," Isabella said.

"This might help." Great Granny Joyce handed Isabella a folder of leaflets about different charities. "The Royal Family are patrons of all these charities and have been for a long time."

Isabella emptied all the leaflets out and got reading. There were so many charities that needed help and support. She narrowed it down to the final four she was most interested in helping and showed her Great Granny.

"Excellent choices, sweetheart."

Friends of the Elderly

Friends of the Elderly
This charity focuses on helping elderly people in the community by providing residential care, day care, or just a friendly face when it is needed most. The Queen has been a devoted patron for nearly 70 years.

BookTrust
Founded in 1921, this is the UK's largest children's reading charity, dedicated to helping young people learn to read. Each year, BookTrust helps up to 3.4 million children across the UK with books, resources, and support to help develop a love of reading.

RSPCA
Established in 1824, the Royal Society for the Prevention of Cruelty to Animals (RSPCA) is a charity in England and Wales that protects animals against neglect, cruelty, and abuse. The first patron was Queen Victoria in 1837.

"Right, I've thought long and hard, and I've made my mind up," said Isabella. "I'm going to raise money for all four charities! I'll have a sale of my old clothes at the weekend – stuff that doesn't fit me or I don't wear anymore, and then I'll split the money."

"I am so proud of you. That's a perfect plan!" said Great Granny Joyce, encouragingly.

Save the Children

Save the Children UK
The UK branch of this charity helps children living in poverty, while the international arm operates in 122 countries around the world, giving care and support to children based on their needs, including vaccinations, antibiotics, or setting up help centres after disasters.

Fiji, 1953

Canada, 1970

"The Queen doesn't just care about what's going on in the UK, you know," said Great Granny Joyce. "She has visited countries all over the world. She's been to places in Europe, such as France, Italy, and Turkey, but also to China, Japan, and the USA. And she's made more than 200 trips to different Commonwealth countries, too."

Isabella remembered reading about the Commonwealth and seeing the world map.

"One of Her Majesty's charities is The Queen's Commonwealth Trust, which supports young people of the Commonwealth and helps them as they work to improve their communities."

Malaysia, 1972

"That's incredible! The Queen must have helped so many people in her lifetime! Does she ever meet any of them?" asked Isabella.

"Yes, she does," replied Great Granny Joyce.

"Wow! People must get so excited when The Queen visits. I know I would," continued Isabella.

"They definitely do. Huge crowds gather and flags come out in force. It's a real celebration!"

"Which country is The Queen's favourite?" asked Isabella.

Uganda, 2007

"I don't know! Maybe she doesn't have one. But did you know, The Queen doesn't need a passport to travel?" smiled Great Granny Joyce as she put the map and photographs back in the Treasures Box.

"But doesn't everyone need a passport to travel abroad?" asked Isabella.

"All UK passports are issued in the name of Her Majesty, so she can't really give one to herself!"

They both laughed.

UK passports

Apart from The Queen, everyone in the UK needs a passport to travel abroad. Traditionally, the UK passport was navy blue. In the 1970s, the UK joined countries that had formed an organisation called the European Economic Community, which later became the European Union (EU). Shortly after, British passports were changed to burgundy to match the others in the EU. Then, in 2016, the UK voted to leave the EU. This decision was called "Brexit", which is short for "Britain's Exit". When the UK left in 2020, UK passports went back to being navy blue again.

Isabella arrived at her Great Granny Joyce's house, breathless with excitement. She emptied her bag, grabbed her laptop, and switched it on.

"I've found something you're going to love!"

"Show me!" Great Granny Joyce clapped her hands in delight.

Isabella typed quickly and turned her laptop around to show her great granny.

"I've been doing some research of my own. It turns out The Queen launched her very own website in 1997. Here it is: www.royal.uk."

Great Granny Joyce studied the screen. "Well, I never!"

"This is the Royal website! Have a play around and see what you can find."

Great Granny Joyce was soon in her element. She was scrolling up and down, clicking away, and reading out loud.

"I can't believe it!" she exclaimed. "There are Royal events, ceremonies, and visits, as well as information on the Commonwealth. It's all on there, Isabella! And look at this!"

"What is it?" asked Isabella.

"In 1976, The Queen sent her first email and became the first monarch in history to send one!"

"How does she sign her emails?" thought Isabella out loud.

"'Elizabeth R' it says here. Well, I didn't know that..."

"Neither did I! What does the 'R' mean?
I thought her name was Windsor," said Isabella.

"This site says it stands for 'Regina', which
means 'queen' in Latin. How interesting!"

Isabella smiled. She wondered
if she would ever get her
great granny off the
laptop at this rate!

Eventually, Great Granny Joyce finished browsing the Royal website. It got her thinking.

"Of course, The Queen isn't always on international trips, helping out with disasters, or doing charity work," she pointed out. "She likes to have fun, too. Have you heard of James Bond?"

Isabella rolled her eyes, "Of course! Who hasn't? Mum loves all the Bond films."

"Ooooh yes, there is always plenty of action in those films." Great Granny lifted her cup of tea in the air as if giving a toast to Bond.

"Well, it turns out The Queen is a Bond fan, too. For the 2012 London Olympic Games opening ceremony, The Queen filmed a scene with James Bond – well, actually with Daniel Craig, the actor who played him. In the scene, James Bond visits Buckingham Palace to take Her Majesty to the Olympic Games and they parachute into the stadium."

Isabella listened intently, her eyes like saucers. "You're telling me The Queen arrived by parachute?"

Great Granny Joyce couldn't help but chuckle. "They didn't really parachute in. They used stunt people to do the jumps and make it look like The Queen and James Bond. It was only the real Queen at the beginning and the end of the scene."

"I need to see this! I'll look it up online."

Great Granny Joyce watched her great granddaughter find the clip and play it on her laptop.

Isabella giggled away while watching. "The audience are clapping the whole time. You can hear it all around the stadium. What an amazing atmosphere!"

Going for gold

As well as hosting the 2012 Olympic Games and Paralympic Games, Great Britain was very successful, finishing third in each of the medals tables. Team GB won a total of 65 medals at the Olympics, 29 of which were gold. At the Paralympics for competitors with disabilities, Great Britain won 120 medals, including 34 golds.

Princess Anne rode one of The Queen's horses in an equestrian event at the 1976 Olympics. Her daughter, Zara Phillips, won silver in the same event at the 2012 Olympics!

The Commonwealth Games

The Olympics isn't the only sporting event attended by The Queen. Since 1970, Her Majesty has been present at either the opening or closing ceremony of the Commonwealth Games. Commonwealth countries compete in this spectacular multi-sport event every four years.

Weightlifter **Marcus Stephen** of Nauru, the smallest country in the Commonwealth, has won 12 medals at the Games. This has helped Nauru achieve 22nd place on the all-time Commonwealth Games medal table. Stephen became the 11th President of Nauru in 2007.

Northern Ireland shooter **David Calvert** has made the most appearances at the Commonwealth Games, making his debut in 1978 and participating in his 11th Games in 2018 aged 67.

Australia is one of only six countries to have attended all the Commonwealth Games since the competition began in 1930. It is the most successful nation with more than 2,000 medals, and has hosted the Games a record five times.

At the 2014 Commonwealth Games, held in Glasgow, **Kiribati** won its first ever gold medal in a global sporting event when David Katoatau took top prize in a weightlifting competition.

The 1998 Commonwealth Games, in Malaysia's capital city of **Kuala Lumpur**, was the first to be held in Asia and the first to feature team sports, including cricket, hockey, netball, and rugby.

The **Queen's Baton Relay** marks the official countdown to the start of the Commonwealth Games. The Queen puts a message inside a baton that is carried across the Commonwealth on an epic journey lasting several months. The message is read aloud at the opening ceremony of the Games.

Australian shooter **Phillip Adams** and English shooter **Mick Gault** share the record for the most medals won at the Commonwealth Games with 18 medals each.

Nine nations have hosted the Games since it began in 1930: Australia (five times); Canada (four times); England, Scotland, and New Zealand (three times); India, Jamaica, Malaysia, and Wales (once). In 2022, the Games will be held in **Birmingham**, England.

Gold medal

The Queen's Baton

Chapter Five

Inspiration and Innovation

It was a lovely Sunday afternoon. Great Granny Joyce was serving up curried chickpea and rice as Isabella sat at the table talking to Rhys on a video call.

Great Granny Joyce walked across to Isabella and watched the children with affection as they chatted away. Isabella paused and looked up.

"What are you thinking, Great Granny?"

"Just about how different life is now. You two, chatting away on a computer. When I was your age, I remember it was unusual to have even one phone in the house! We may not have had all the gadgets and gizmos you have today, but we had just as much fun. There were board games to play, trees to climb, and songs to sing. As we grew up, things began to change. New inventions appeared, things that transformed our daily lives – things that you, of course, accept as normal now. Life became very exciting."

"What changes did you notice as you grew up?" asked Rhys on the laptop screen.

Great Granny gestured round the kitchen and living room with her arms.

"At first, it was mainly household goods. The Queen and I were born in 1926, the same year that the TV was invented. That was big news! It changed entertainment for everyone. Winston and I had to save up for a long time to afford one."

The children laughed at Great Granny's enthusiasm. They both took television totally for granted.

"When we got married, Winston and I worked hard and saved up to buy things for our home. We bought a washing machine, a fridge, and a vacuum cleaner. All those time-saving devices made a big difference to our lives."

Isabella nodded, mesmerised by the changes that her great granny had witnessed.

"And I remember the day we got a toaster! Well, it was the best thing since sliced bread!" Great Granny Joyce said with a chuckle.

"What about outside the home? What other things have happened?" asked Isabella.

"Well, travel by planes, boats, and trains has become easier, cheaper, and quicker over the years. People have even been into space! Medical marvels keep people healthy and new technology has changed how we live. The world is a different place today."

A century of innovation

This timeline shows some incredible inventions and achievements by creative geniuses from the UK and Commonwealth countries during The Queen's lifetime.

> I remember having antibiotics when I wasn't well – they really worked. Thank you, Mr Fleming!

1926
Television
Scottish inventor John Logie Baird demonstrated moving television images, which evolved into the home entertainment systems we see today.

1928
Penicillin discovery
Scottish scientist Alexander Fleming noticed that mould was destroying bacteria in his laboratory, and used this to create the first antibiotic. Since the 1940s, penicillin has saved the lives of millions.

1930
Jet engine
English engineer Sir Frank Whittle patented his design for a jet engine. The first successful flight of a British jet aircraft took off in 1941.

1951
Zebra crossing
The first zebra crossing was installed in Slough, England. Vehicles had to stop at these black-and-white striped road markings, so pedestrians could cross the road safely.

1978
Bionic ear
Australian professor Graeme Clark invented the the cochlear implant – an electronic device that is placed inside the ear, and which helps people who have hearing loss to understand sound.

1987
Sight-saving medicine
Jamaican researchers Professor Manley West and Dr Albert Lockhart developed Canasol, a treatment for glaucoma, a serious eye condition, saving the sight of people all over the world.

1989
World Wide Web
English inventor Tim Berners-Lee invented the World Wide Web (www) – the system of linked web pages with comprehensive content for the public to access through the internet.

1996
Wind-up radio
English inventor Trevor Baylis designed the wind-up radio, powered by a handheld crank. This meant that people without access to power could access news and information.

1996
Animal cloning
Scientists at the Roslin Institute, University of Edinburgh, created Dolly the sheep, cloned from her parent sheep as an identical copy. This made Dolly the first-ever cloned mammal.

1953
DNA structure
English biologist Francis Crick and US scientist James Watson used the work of English chemist Rosalind Franklin as the basis for their structure of DNA – the genetic code for all living things – and won the Nobel Prize for their efforts.

1955
Hovercraft
English engineer Christopher Sydney Cockerell invented the hovercraft, a high-speed water vehicle that hovers over the sea on a cushion of air, like a giant inflatable tyre.

1959
Mini
This classic compact car was created by English inventor Alec Issigonis. The attractive design, small size, and affordable price tag made the Mini hugely popular.

1965
Portable defibrillator
Northern Ireland cardiologist Frank Pantridge invented the portable defibrillator, an emergency device that helps failing hearts, and has since saved millions of lives.

1967
Supersize screens
Canadian filmmakers Graeme Ferguson, Roman Kroitor, Robert Kerr, and William Shaw gave movie-goers a new experience with giant, high-definition IMAX screens, six times bigger than standard screens.

1997
Harry Potter
The first book about fictitious wizard Harry Potter, entitled *Harry Potter and the Philosopher's Stone*, was published. This led to seven books by English writer J. K. Rowling in the best-selling series, as well as a successful film franchise.

2007
iPhone
English–American Jony Ive helped to revolutionise mobile phones when he designed the stylish iPhone with its touch screen, lightweight frame, and built-in mobile App Store. He also designed the iPad, iPod, and Apple Watch.

2015
Space visit
English astronaut Tim Peake became the first British astronaut to visit the International Space Station (ISS) and the first person to be awarded an honour from The Queen while in space.

2021
Space tourism
On board his Virgin Galactic rocket plane, English entrepreneur Richard Branson flew into space for an hour-long trip of a lifetime, paving the way for tourists to visit space in the future.

How exciting, a trip to space! I wonder if there's room for me on the next flight?

When Isabella had finished talking to her cousin, she shut her laptop and followed her great granny over to the Treasures Box. Great Granny Joyce continued, "There have been so many amazing achievements around the world as Her Majesty The Queen and I have grown older!"

Great Granny Joyce took a handful of postcards from the box and showed them to Isabella. "Every time something happened that impressed or inspired me, I bought a postcard and put it in the box. Look at all of these incredible events and inventions,"

Great Granny Joyce inspected the first postcard. "Ooh, look at the England football team at Wembley after their victory in 1966. The Queen handed the trophy to the captain Bobby Moore. So far, it's the only time England has won the World Cup."

"I can't wait to watch the World Cup this year!" grinned Isabella. "Lots of my favourite players from all over the world will be playing."

The next postcard was a picture of the 1969 Moon landing. Isabella had learned about this at school. US astronauts Neil Armstrong and Buzz Aldrin, two crew members on the Apollo 11 space mission, made history as the first people to walk on the Moon.

"I remember that day so well. More than 600 million people were watching around the world. Did you know the Apollo 11 astronauts visited The Queen at Buckingham Palace three months later?"

Isabella and Great Granny Joyce got to their feet and both pretended to be on the Moon, moving around really slowly and lifting their legs as high as they could, which wasn't very high in Great Granny Joyce's case!

Great Granny Joyce paused for breath and said, "And you know, 22 years after the Moon landing, in 1991, Helen Sharman became the first British person to travel into space."

"That's amazing!" exclaimed Isabella. She held out a new postcard. "What about this one?"

"That one is the Channel Tunnel. Starting in 1988, more than 13,000 builders took five years to create this huge tunnel under the sea, going all the way from England to France. It really is a miracle of engineering!"

"I remember it now," said Isabella. "I went through the Channel Tunnel to France on holiday!"

Isabella put the postcards back in the box and sighed. "It's so inspiring seeing what people can achieve. I wonder what I'll achieve..."

Great Granny Joyce put an arm around her great granddaughter's shoulder. "Wonderful things, sweetheart, wonderful things."

"Do you remember when you read about how The Queen works with the government? Well, Her Majesty has been on the throne for so long that she has seen 14 prime ministers take charge!"

"I know who the current Prime Minister is!" remembered Isabella.

"I know you do, but there have been many others. You can see them all on your tablet, I'm sure," Great Granny Joyce suggested.

Isabella got busy looking up the British prime ministers who had served alongside The Queen.

"Is The Queen friends with all the prime ministers?" asked Isabella.

"It's more of a working relationship. Every week, The Queen has a meeting with the Prime Minister."

"What do they talk about?" wondered Isabella.

"No one knows. The conversations are strictly confidential. I expect they talk about the important issues of the week and discuss whatever is happening around the country at the time," smiled Great Granny Joyce.

Prime ministers since 1940

Winston Churchill
1940–1945 and
1951–1955

Clement Attlee
1945–1951

Harold Wilson
1964–1970 and
1974–1976

Edward Heath
1970–1974

Tony Blair
1997–2007

Gordon Brown
2007–2010

Anthony Eden
1955–1957

Harold Macmillan
1957–1963

Alec Douglas-Home
1963–1964

James Callaghan
1976–1979

Margaret Thatcher
1979–1990

John Major
1990–1997

David Cameron
2010–2016

Theresa May
2016–2019

Boris Johnson
2019–present

What does devolution mean?

The UK government, based in the Houses of Parliament in London, is responsible for things like foreign affairs that run hroughout the UK. In Scotland, Wales, and Northern Ireland, other things, such as education and transport, are the responsibility of the devolved governments. This is called devolution, which means that decisions can be taken in places that are closer to the people they affect. The heads of the devolved governments are called first ministers, not prime ministers. England does not have a separate government and is run by the UK government, but some decisions are now made by city mayors.

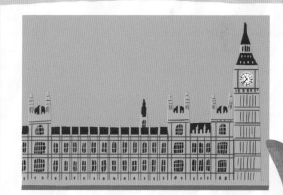

Houses of Parliament, London

Once they had finished talking about prime ministers, Isabella settled down with Tiger.

"I've heard that extraordinary people can be recognised by The Queen. Men are given a knighthood and women receive a damehood," recalled Isabella.

"You're quite right," agreed Great Granny Joyce. "A knighthood or damehood is one of the greatest titles that The Queen can give anyone. In medieval times, knighthoods were given to the bravest soldiers in battle. It's called the honours system. Men are called Sir, while women are named Dame."

"That sounds very special!"

"Yes, it is special. People receive their knighthood or damehood in a ceremony attended by The Queen or another Member of the Royal Family," explained Great Granny Joyce.

"Other honours, such as the OBE, MBE, CBE, and BEM, are also given to acknowledge people's achievements, Isabella. That lovely footballer Marcus Rashford received an MBE for his work in supporting children who live in poverty," Great Granny continued.

"I have his book *You Are a Champion* at home!" exclaimed Isabella.

Film and TV

Dame Maggie Smith
English actress Maggie Smith received a damehood for services to acting in 1990. She has played Minerva McGonagall in the *Harry Potter* film series, as well as Violet Crawley in *Downton Abbey*.

Sir Lenny Henry
English comedian and co-founder of Comic Relief, a UK charity that has raised more than £1 billion in the fight against poverty, Lenny Henry received his knighthood in 2015.

Sport

Dame Tanni Grey-Thompson
Welsh wheelchair racer Tanni Grey-Thompson was awarded a damehood in 2005 in recognition of her 11 gold medals at the Paralympic Games.

Sir Andy Murray
Scottish tennis player Andy Murray has won two Olympic gold medals and, in 2013, he was the first British player in 77 years to win the Wimbledon men's singles title. He was knighted in 2017.

Sir Mo Farah
Somali-born English long-distance runner Mo Farah has won four Olympic gold medals and received a knighthood in 2017 for his services to athletics.

Lady Mary Peters
Northern Ireland athlete Mary Peters won the gold medal in the pentathlon at the 1972 Olympics and bagged three Commonwealth Games gold medals before being given a damehood in 2000.

Music

Sir Elton John

English singer–songwriter Elton John has released more than 30 albums and sold 300 million records. He received a knighthood for his services to music and charity in 1998.

Dame Olivia Newton-John

English–Australian singer and actor Olivia Newton-John was awarded a damehood in 2020 for her services to entertainment, charity, and cancer research.

My favourite is Sir David Attenborough. I love watching the animals in his TV programmes.

Dame Shirley Bassey

Welsh singer Shirley Bassey, famously known as the voice behind three of the James Bond theme songs, received her damehood in 1999.

Design

Dame Zaha Hadid

Iraqi-born British architect Zaha Hadid, best known for her futuristic designs, including the Heydar Aliyev Center in Baku, Azerbaijan, and the London Aquatics Centre, received her damehood in 2012.

Dame Vivienne Westwood

For decades, English fashion designer Vivienne Westwood has turned the fashion world on its head with her bold catwalk creations, resulting in a damehood in 2006.

Science

Sir David Attenborough

English conservationist, biologist, and broadcaster David Attenborough is the only person ever to have received two knighthoods – in 1985 and 2020.

Sir Chris Whitty

England's Chief Medical Officer Chris Whitty took a major role in managing the COVID-19 pandemic, including giving regular updates at televised press conferences. He was knighted in 2022.

A great choice. His programmes are excellent, aren't they?

Dame Jane Goodall

Known for her environmental and humanitarian work, English anthropologist and primatologist Jane Goodall received her damehood in 2004.

Dame Sarah Gilbert

English vaccinologist Sarah Gilbert has helped to create groundbreaking vaccines against influenza and COVID-19, earning her a damehood in 2021.

Young heroes

The Queen doesn't just honour famous faces. Her Majesty has also rewarded thousands of ordinary people who have proved themselves to be extraordinary. Meet some of the amazing young people honoured by The Queen for making a real difference to our world...

British Empire Medal

Tobias Weller was 11 when he became the youngest person ever awarded a British Empire Medal (BEM). Tobias has cerebral palsy and completed two marathons and raised £150,000 for charities.

In 2018, a 14-year-old hero named **Joe Rowlands** received a Queen's Commendation for Bravery after he saved his father from drowning when their kayak capsized at sea.

During the COVID-19 pandemic, A-level student **Muhammad Kamil Ali** gave free tuition to young people struggling with school closures. He was awarded a BEM for his generous gesture.

Alexia Hilbertidou received a Queen's Young Leaders Award in 2018 for setting up an organisation to help girls succeed in mathematics, technology, and business.

13-year-old **Jonjo Heuerman** raised money for cancer research by cycling thousands of miles around Britain. He received a BEM in 2016 for his pedal power.

Alimatu Bawah Wiabriga received a Queen's Young Leaders Award in 2018 for developing an ingenious app called CowTribe to help farmers in Ghana care for their livestock by giving them easier access to vets.

Stephen Sutton was diagnosed with cancer, and became a blogger and fundraiser who helped raise £5 million for the Teenage Cancer Trust charity. After Stephen's death at the age of 19, the Queen awarded him an MBE.

Aged 24, **Amelia Collins-Patel** received an MBE after arranging chat sessions for young people who felt lonely during COVID-19 lockdowns.

Max Woosey was only 10 years old when he began camping to raise money for his local hospice. During 640 nights spent camping, Max pitched his tent at London Zoo and the Prime Minister's garden at 10 Downing Street. He received a BEM for his outdoor efforts.

Chapter Six
Celebration and Commemoration

Great Granny Joyce was a ball of excitement. She couldn't sit still. Her eyes shone and she kept checking all the memorabilia in the Treasures Box as if to make sure it was all still there.

"I can't believe the Jubilee is this weekend! We've been looking forward to it for such a long time."

Considering everything she had learned from Great Granny Joyce and her Treasures Box, Isabella felt the same.

"I looked on the Royal website and there's so much going on," declared Isabella.

"For starters, there is a longer bank holiday to allow for four days of celebrations! You know we love a party!" squealed Great Granny Joyce.

Isabella smiled. "There is The Queen's Birthday Parade with more than 1,000 soldiers, and a special service giving thanks for The Queen's reign at St Paul's Cathedral. Sandringham House and Balmoral Castle will be open to visitors, and The Queen will attend the Derby at Epsom Downs during the Jubilee weekend."

"Of course, Her Majesty wouldn't miss the horse racing!" Great Granny Joyce pointed out.

Isabella nodded. "Then there is the royal tradition of lighting beacons all over the UK and the Commonwealth countries."

"How magical!" exclaimed Great Granny Joyce. "Don't forget there is the Platinum Party at the Palace with a live concert broadcast from Buckingham Palace."

"Wow! Imagine getting tickets for that!"

"Don't worry, Isabella. Lots of people in the UK will be celebrating with street parties, picnics, and garden barbecues. And remember, you're invited to my Joyful Jubilee Lunch."

"Thank you," laughed Isabella. "I accept your invitation!"

"Let's start making new flags and bunting," said Great Granny Joyce. "The countdown begins now..."

It was the day of the Joyful Jubilee Lunch! Everyone was there, including Isabella's family and her cousin Rhys. Even Tiger made an appearance.

Great Granny Joyce toasted The Queen, "To Her Majesty on her 70th Jubilee!"

As the guests tucked into the food, Great Granny Joyce called Isabella over.

"I've got you something special for the Jubilee..."

Isabella smiled in anticipation.

From behind her back, Great Granny pulled out a sparkling little box!

"This is for you. It's about time you had your own Treasures Box to fill."

Isabella was speechless. She took the lid off and looked inside.
In the box was a single postcard, a stunning portrait of The Queen.
On the back, in Great Granny Joyce's familiar handwriting, were the words:

"My dear Great Granddaughter Isabella, may you fill up your own
Treasures Box with a lifetime of happy memories."

Isabella was thrilled. Her eyes shone with tears of happiness.
She hugged her great granny tighter than ever before.

The first memory Isabella was going to add to her box was a souvenir
from the 2022 Jubilee. She would fill up her Treasures Box just like her
Great Granny Joyce had done over so many years. History was repeating
itself in the most wonderful way. Isabella couldn't wait to start her own
collection of magic memories and treasured times...

In Her Majesty's own words...

"Family does not necessarily mean blood relatives but often a description of a community, organisation, or nation."

"When life seems hard, the courageous do not lie down and accept defeat; instead, they are all the more determined to struggle for a better future."

I cannot lead you into battle. I do not give you laws or administer justice but I can do something else - I can give my heart and my devotion to these old islands and to all the peoples of our brotherhood of nations.

"Cowards falter, but danger is often overcome by those who nobly dare."

"I have to be seen to be believed."

"The lessons from the peace process are clear; whatever life throws at us, our individual responses will be all the stronger for working together and sharing the load."

"It has been women who have breathed gentleness and care into the harsh progress of mankind."

February... will see the start of my Platinum Jubilee year, which I hope will be an opportunity for people everywhere to enjoy a sense of togetherness; a chance to give thanks for the enormous changes of the last 70 years – social, scientific, and cultural – and also to look ahead with confidence.

"Good memories are our second chance at happiness."

Find out more

Castles, palaces, stately homes, and museums all around the UK chronicle its rich heritage. Their websites also help us to learn about the past in more depth and detail. Many of the places featured here are open to visitors, but check opening times before you visit as some are not open all year round.

England

Jorvik Viking Centre, York

Journey through this reconstruction of the Viking city of Jorvik and experience the sights and smells of life 1,000 years ago.

Osborne House, Isle of Wight

Explore the stunning holiday home of Queen Victoria and Prince Albert.

Hever Castle, Kent

Once the childhood home of Anne Boleyn, this beautiful moated castle has 700 years of history to uncover.

Buckingham Palace, London

This magnificent palace has been the official London residence of the UK's monarchs since 1837.

Beamish, County Durham

A world-famous open-air museum that shows what everyday life was like in the north of England at the height of the industrial age.

Wales

Big Pit National Coal Museum, Torfaen

Including underground tours of a real coal mine, this is the perfect place to explore the history of coal and industry in South Wales.

Conwy Castle, North Wales

A magnificent medieval castle built in the 13th century by Edward I.

Ffestiniog Railway, Gwynedd

This historic railway travels through the spectacular Snowdonia National Park.

Harlech Castle, Harlech

One of Edward I's mighty fortresses, this castle has played an important role in many wars, from the Wars of the Roses to the English Civil War.

Castell Henllys Iron Age Village, Pembrokeshire

Travel back in time to an authentic Iron Age village.

Scotland

Dunfermline Abbey and Palace, Fife
This impressive palace was once home to many Scots Royals, and is the burial site of Robert the Bruce.

Stirling Castle, Stirling
Located on a steep clifftop, the childhood home of Mary, Queen of Scots has 500 years of dramatic history.

Palace of Holyroodhouse, Edinburgh
Located on Edinburgh's Royal Mile, this is The Queen's official residence in Scotland, and the home of Scottish royal history.

Glasgow Science Centre
Opened by The Queen in 2001, this centre has three floors featuring more than 250 scientific exhibits.

Skara Brae, Orkney
This is the site of Europe's best preserved Neolithic village. Dating back 5,000 years, it's even older than Stonehenge!

Northern Ireland

Titanic Belfast
This museum tells the story of RMS *Titanic*, the ship that sank after hitting an iceberg on its maiden voyage in 1912.

Carrick-a-Rede, County Antrim
Swaying high above the Atlantic Ocean, this rope bridge has linked Carrick-a-Rede Island to the mainland for more than 250 years.

Ulster Folk Museum, Holywood
Explore cottages, farms, schools, and shops just as they were more than 100 years ago in Ulster.

Navan Centre & Fort, Armagh
This hilltop site once housed an ancient temple, and is one of Northern Ireland's most important archaeological attractions.

Enniskillen Castle Museums, County Fermanagh
Built almost 600 years ago, Enniskillen Castle was once the home of ruling Irish tribe the Maguires. It now includes the Fermanagh County Museum and the Inniskillings Museum.

The Queen in numbers

As The Queen celebrates 70 years on the throne, here is a look at her life in numbers.

2 **birthdays** a year

0 **passports** needed to travel

12 great **grandchildren**

25 the age **Princess Elizabeth** became **Queen**

1 personal **bagpiper**

17 **ships** launched

1,500 **Christmas puddings** given each year to staff as gifts from The Queen

73 years married to **Prince Philip**

The Queen has sat for about **200** portraits

4.2 million items of **mail** received

Important words and ideas

abdication

when a monarch gives up being king or queen

Angles

people from north Germany who settled in England in the fifth and sixth centuries

Anglo-Saxons

the people who ruled England from 410 to 1066. They were a mixture of different peoples from northern Europe who, over time, mixed with the people who were already in England

antibiotics

a type of medicine that destroys bacteria and stops infections

apartheid

a system that existed in South Africa in which black people did not have the same rights as white people. Black and white people lived, worked, and studied separately due to racial segregation, which means separating people in daily life, based on their race

bank holiday

a public holiday in the UK. The Platinum Jubilee bank holidays are on 2 June and 3 June 2022

beacons

lights or fires on a hill or tower, used as a warning or celebration

BEM

British Empire Medal. An honour awarded for "hands-on" service to the community

British Empire

the group of countries and territories that were once ruled by Britain. The British Empire began in the 16th century and, over time, Britain took over many nations. By the 20th century, many countries in the Empire wished to be independent. After independence, some countries kept a connection to the UK by joining the Commonwealth, which came into existence in 1931. Unlike the British Empire, the Commonwealth is a voluntary and equal group of countries

CBE

Commander of the Order of the British Empire. An honour given to those who have made an exceptional achievement or improved the lives of others through their service. It is the highest Order of the British Empire

Church of England

the main Christian church in England. The Queen is the Head of the Church of England

civil war

a war between groups of people in one country

climate change

changes to the Earth's temperature and weather over a long period of time. This is happening more quickly because humans burn fossil fuels, such as oil, gas, and coal

commemoration

remembering an important person or event with a ceremony or a special object, such as a coin

Commonwealth

an organisation made up of the UK and many of the countries that were once part of the British Empire. There are 54 independent and equal members

conservation

protection of the planet, particularly nature

coronation

a ceremony where a person is crowned king or queen

COVID-19

a type of coronavirus that causes breathing difficulties. It was first seen in 2019 and led to a pandemic, affecting the whole world. In 2022, the pandemic is ongoing

democratic

description of a country that is ruled by a government voted for by the people; the people vote anonymously and are free to vote for the leader or government they like

discrimination

unfair treatment of a person or group of people, based on prejudices (ideas that are not based on facts) about who they are, or the way they look or act. People can be discriminated against for many reasons, including their race, religion, or gender

donation

money or gifts given to help a person or organisation

entrepreneur

a person who starts their own business

European Union (EU)

a group of European countries that makes shared decisions on economic and political plans and policies. The UK left the EU in 2020

famine

a major food shortage that causes many people to die

fortifications

buildings or walls built to protect a place from attack

Gaelic games

traditional sports that are played in the Republic of Ireland and Northern Ireland, and around the world

general election

a vote by the people of a country to decide who will form the government and run the country

government

a group of people that run the country and make the laws

Green Belt Movement

an environmental group based in Kenya. "Green belt" refers to areas of countryside that cannot be built upon

Highland Games

events that take place in Scotland featuring traditional sports, dancing, and music

honours system

honours are awarded to people, organisations, or countries that have achieved great things or given exceptional service. The most well-known honours include knighthood, damehood, CBE, OBE, MBE, and BEM

humanitarian

concerned with improving peoples' lives and preventing suffering

influenza

more commonly known as flu, an illness that is similar to a bad cold with aching muscles

Jubilee

the anniversary of a major event. 2022 is the Platinum Jubilee year, marking 70 years of The Queen's reign

line of Succession

the line of Succession shows who will become monarch when a reigning monarch dies or stops being the ruler. His Royal Highness The Prince of Wales is first in the UK's line of Succession

Magna Carta

a document signed in 1215, which stated that monarchs must obey the law of the land. This marked a new era, where the monarch was no longer totally in charge

MBE

Member of the Order of the British Empire. An honour given to those who have achieved great things or given exceptional service. It is the third highest Order of the British Empire

Members of Parliament

known as MPs, people elected to Parliament to represent an area or region

monarch

a king, queen, emperor, or empress. The position of monarch is passed down from one member of a royal family to another

National Anthem

a nation's official song, played on public occasions such as major sports events

National Health Service (NHS)

a UK service, formed in 1948, that provides medical services, such as treatment for illness, vaccinations, and operations. Individual people don't pay when they use the service. Instead, money from taxes funds most of the NHS

Nobel Peace Prize

an annual prize awarded to a person or organisation that has done important work towards peace. There are other Nobel Prizes, including one for medicine

Normans

people from northern France who invaded England and Wales in the 11th century

OBE

an Officer of the Order of the British Empire. An honour given to those who have achieved great things or given exceptional service. It is the second highest Order of the British Empire

Olympic Games

a group of international sports competitions that takes place once every four years, in a different country each time. Athletes compete for their country

pandemic

describes a disease that affects many people across a wide area. Since 2019, the world has been experiencing the COVID-19 pandemic

Paralympic Games

a group of international sports competitions for people with disabilities that takes place once every four years, in a different country each time. Athletes compete for their country

parliament

a group of people, usually elected, who make the laws for a country or region

patent

the legal right to be the only person to make or sell an invention for a certain amount of time

Picts

the group of people who lived in what is now north-east Scotland during Roman times

prime minister

the leader of the government in certain countries, including the UK

reign

to rule a country as king or queen

Roman Empire

the countries that ancient Rome ruled from 27 BC until AD 476. These countries included Britain, France, and Spain. The Roman Empire was the largest empire in the ancient world

Saxons

people from northern Germany who settled in England in the fifth and sixth centuries

Sherpa

a member of a people from the Himalayan region of Asia

Spanish Armada

the fleet of 130 Spanish ships sent to invade England in 1588. England defeated the fleet

tamarind ball

a sweet-and-sour snack made from tamarind fruit and sugar. Tamarind balls are popular throughout the Caribbean

trinkets

small objects or pieces of jewellery that do not cost very much money

United Nations (UN)

an international organisation, founded in 1945 after World War II ended, to encourage peace and cooperation throughout the world

Vikings

a group of people from Scandinavia who travelled by sea and raided other parts of Europe. Between the 8th and 11th centuries, Vikings settled in some of the countries they invaded

war veterans

people who have served in the armed forces during a war or conflict

World War I

a war fought mainly in Europe and the Middle East that involved more than 30 countries, and took place between 1914 and 1918. Up until that time, it was the world's most destructive war, and around 40 million people died

World War II

the biggest war in history, which took place between 1939 and 1945. More than 30 countries were involved. The war was fought between two groups: the Allied Powers (including the UK, France, the Soviet Union, the United States of America, and China) and the Axis Powers (including Germany, Italy, and Japan). A total of about 75 million people died

Index

DK | Penguin
Random
House

DK has brought together an expert creative team to deliver this celebratory book about our Queen, in honour of her Platinum Jubilee. Educators and history experts from across the UK and Commonwealth have collaborated to supplement the warm, inclusive story, working with illustrators, designers, and editors to put together the ultimate guide to Queen Elizabeth and her reign for children, working closely with the Department for Education and Royal Collection Trust at every stage of the book's creation.

DK would like to thank the many people who have contributed their precious time to this landmark project. Those who have written and illustrated for the pages of this book, we couldn't have done this without you and you know who you are - thank you. Without your knowledge, talent, dedication, and expertise, this book that will be memorable to so many children wouldn't be as special as it is.

First published in Great Britain in 2022 by
Dorling Kindersley Limited
DK, One Embassy Gardens, 8 Viaduct Gardens,
London, SW11 7BW

The authorised representative in the EEA is
Dorling Kindersley Verlag GmbH. Arnulfstr. 124,
80636 Munich, Germany

Copyright © 2022 Dorling Kindersley Limited
A Penguin Random House Company

The QR code on this page will take you to:
https://jubilee.dk.com/
For details on how your data will be used,
please see the site privacy policy:
https://jubilee.dk.com/privacy.html

Printed and bound in Italy
by L.E.G.O. S.p.A.

For the curious
www.dk.com

MIX
Paper | Supporting
responsible forestry
FSC™ C018179

This book was made with Forest Stewardship Council™ certified paper – one small step in DK's commitment to a sustainable future. For more information go to www.dk.com/our-green-pledge

Scan this QR code
to access the audio
book and more.